W9-DFM-498

NEW WORLD CONTINENTS & LAND BRIDGES

North and South America

Continents

Bruce McClish

Heinemann Library
Chicago, Illinois

Designed by Stella Vassiliou
Maps and diagrams by Pat Kermode and Stella Vassiliou
Printed in China by Wing King Tong Co. Ltd.

07 06 05 04 03
10 9 8 7 6 5 4 3 2 1

Library of Congress Cataloging-in-Publication Data
McClish, Bruce.
  New world continents and land bridges : North and South America /
Bruce McClish.
     v. cm. -- (Continents)
Summary: The Americas -- Introducing North America -- North America: landforms -- North America: climate, plants and animals -- North America: history and culture -- Introducing South America -- South America: landforms -- South America: climate, plants and animals -- South America: history and culture -- Continental connections and plate tectonics -- Land bridges: the narrow link -- Land bridges: dropping seas.
Includes bibliographical references (p.   ).
  ISBN 1-4034-2988-X (lib. bdg. : hardcover) 1-4034-4246-0 (paperback)
 1. North America--Juvenile literature. 2. South America--Juvenile literature. 3. Continents--Juvenile literature. [1. North America. 2. South America. 3. Continents.] I. Title. II. Continents (Chicago, Ill.)

 G639.4 .M33 2003
 917--dc21

                              2002011596

Acknowledgments
The author and publishers are grateful to the following for permission to reproduce copyright material:
p. 5 (top) Australian Picture Library/Corbis © NASA; p. 5 (bottom) Australian Picture Library/Corbis © Philip Gould; pp. 7, 8, 9, 10, 11, 18, 27 PhotoDisc; p. 12 Australian Picture Library/Corbis © Joseph Sohm; pp. 13, 21 Australian Picture Library/Corbis © Danny Lehman; p. 15 (top) AUSCAPE/Francois Gohier; p. 15 (bottom) Australian Picture Library/Corbis © Fulvio Roiter; p. 16 (left) Australian Picture Library/Corbis © Wolfgang Kaehler; pp. 16 (right), 25 Australian Picture Library/Corbis © Jay Dickman; p. 17 Australian Picture Library/Corbis © Marko Modic; p. 19 Australian Picture Library/Corbis © Nik Wheeler; p. 22 ANT Photo Library/Pavel German; p. 29 Australian Picture Library/Corbis © Kevin Fleming.

Cover photograph of Death Valley, California, and market in Ecuador supplied by PhotoDisc.

Every effort has been made to contact copyright holders of any material reproduced in this book. Any omissions will be rectified in subsequent printings if notice is given to the publisher.

The author would like to thank: Avi Olshina, geologist; Peter Nunan, geography teacher; Craig Campbell, researcher; and Jenny McClish, researcher and contributing author.

Some words are shown in bold, **like this.** You can find out what they mean by looking in the glossary.

Contents

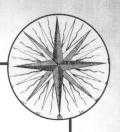

THE AMERICAS

A continent is a huge **landmass** on Earth's surface. We generally speak of seven continents: Europe, Asia, Africa, North America, South America, Australia, and Antarctica. Each continent has big differences from the others in its shape, size, **climate,** plants, animals, and human **cultures.**

On the other hand, some continents have many traits in common and are often associated with each other. North America and South America are two such continents. They are the only continents that share part of their name and are even grouped together as "the Americas." They are also known as New World continents. This is not because the Americas are younger than the other continents. It is because the people who gave this name to the Americas were from Europe. When European **civilization** came to North and South America, they already knew about the Old World continents of Europe, Asia, and Africa. When they discovered that North and South America existed, they called them the New World.

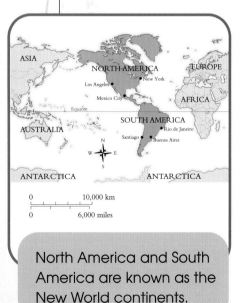

North America and South America are known as the New World continents.

New World links

There are very good reasons for grouping North America and South America together. The two continents are linked by Panama, a country in Central America that forms a narrow **isthmus.** Both continents have large mountain ranges on their western sides and large lowland regions on their eastern sides. They share many kinds of animals, such as armadillos, opossums, jaguars, cougars, and vampire bats. They also have similarities in human culture, such as the Spanish language, which people speak in both North and South America.

Land bridges

The Isthmus of Panama is an example of a land bridge—an area of land that connects two continents. A land bridge makes it easier for plants, animals, and people to cross over into different continents.

Land bridges are not always permanent. They may change, disappear, or reappear over a period of time. For example, the land bridge formed by the Isthmus of Panama was not there more than three million years ago.

Land bridges can be a variety of shapes and sizes. Dozens of land bridges have linked different continents at different times during the past billions of years.

Central America and Latin America

Central America is a narrow area of land between Mexico and South America. Central America, which has seven countries in it, is often referred to as a region on its own. But Central America is not a separate continent. It is part of North America.

A much wider area, shared by both continents is called Latin America. All of the Americas south of the United States—including Mexico, Central America and South America—forms Latin America. In this region, most people speak Spanish or Portuguese and follow the Catholic religion.

North and South America are linked by the narrow Isthmus of Panama.

This all Saints Day ceremony in Louisiana demonstrates just one of the many religions in North and South America.

Introducing
NORTH AMERICA

North America is the third-largest continent. Only Africa and Asia are larger. No other continent has a wider variety of landforms and **climates**—including **polar** mountains, **fertile** plains, scorched deserts, **tropical** beaches, and green forests.

The name *America,* though often used in reference to the United States, can actually refer to any part of North or South America. North America includes Canada, Greenland, Mexico, the United States, and the countries in Central America and the Caribbean. Of the more than fifteen countries in North America, Canada is the largest. The United States is the second largest. Many of the countries are islands, such as Cuba, Jamaica, and Greenland. Most of the countries in North America are small and are located in the tropical tip formed by Central America.

North America is made up of a number of different countries.

Arctic Ocean

GREENLAND

USA

CANADA

Vancouver

UNITED STATES OF AMERICA

Denver

New York

Washington DC

Atlantic Ocean

Los Angeles

Pacific Ocean

Miami

BAHAMAS

MEXICO

CUBA

HAITI

DOMINICAN REPUBLIC

JAMAICA

Mexico City

BELIZE

GUATEMALA

HONDURAS

EL SALVADOR

NICARAGUA

COSTA RICA

PANAMA

N
W E
S

0   2,000 km

North America: facts and figures

Area: 9.4 million sq mi (24.4 million sq km)

Climate: temperate; some polar/tropical areas

Population: 495,369,000

Biggest country: Canada 3.9 million sq mi (10 million sq km)

Highest peak: Mt. McKinley—20,322 ft (6,194 m) above sea level

Lowest point: Death Valley, California—282 ft (86 m) below sea level

Largest freshwater lake: Lake Superior—31,815 sq mi (82,400 sq km)

Longest river: Missouri River—2,684 mi (4,320 km)

Biggest desert: Greenland—840,000 sq mi (2.2 million sq km)

Crop products: wheat, corn, oats, rice, cotton, soybeans, flaxseed, **sorghum**, citrus fruits, (beef and dairy), pigs, sheep, chickens, eggs, fish

Animal and animal products: beef and dairy cattle, pigs, sheep, chickens, eggs, fish

Mineral products: coal, petroleum, natural gas, uranium, gold, silver, nickel, copper, zinc, lead, **iron ore**, phosphate, molybdenum

Manufactured products: automobiles and automobile parts, electronic equipment, aircraft, chemicals, iron and steel, cement, fertilizer, paper products

North America has the world's largest island, Greenland; the largest freshwater lake, Lake Superior; and the tallest type of tree, the California redwood. It is the wealthiest continent, rich in **natural resources** such as water, soil, **timber,** and minerals. It has many businesses and industries, and millions of North Americans enjoy the world's highest **standard of living**.

Summer temperatures in Death Valley often reach over 120 °F (49 °C).

Landforms

North America is shaped roughly like a giant triangle. The western part of the continent has the highest mountains and the driest deserts. The eastern part has lower mountains, bigger lakes, and wider plains. The northern part of the continent is the coldest, and is cut by a great number of bays and inlets.

Highlands and lowlands

The Rocky Mountains, also called the Rockies, are North America's longest mountain range. They reach from Alaska in the north all the way down to Mexico in the south. The eastern side of the Rockies rises sharply, forming a great wall that overlooks neighboring plains. Two other great ranges are the Sierra Nevada of California and the Sierra Madre of Mexico. Many large desert regions lie between North America's western mountain ranges.

The western part of North America has the highest mountains, such as the Grand Tetons.

The Appalachian Mountains are one of the few great ranges on the eastern side of North America. These mountains are older and more worn down than the mountains in the West. North American mountains have been a major source of mineral wealth, including gold, silver, and coal.

East of the Rockies lie North America's great inland plains, or prairie regions. These include a vast region of ranches and farmland stretching across the middle of the continent. More **fertile** lowlands are found closer to the East Coast. The ancient, rocky northeastern part of the continent also has many low-lying regions. The land has mineral wealth, but is poor for farming. This region is known as the Canadian Shield. A shield is the **exposed** core of a continent and contains ancient rocks.

Waterways

Many of North America's low-lying regions were worn down by giant **glaciers** during the **Ice Age**. These glaciers also formed basins for the continent's biggest lakes. The Great Lakes that lie between Canada and the United States form the largest fresh surface water system on Earth. The Great Lakes and all the waterways that connect them to the ocean form one of the main business and industrial centers of North America.

North America's longest rivers flow east of the Rockies and across the wide lowlands. These include the Mississippi and the Missouri Rivers. West of the Rockies, rivers are more likely to flow through spectacular canyons. The Yukon, Columbia, Colorado, Snake, and Rio Grande are some of North America's western rivers.

Diary of a continent

▶ **300 million years ago:**
Coal-age swamps cover much of the continent.

▶ **250 million years ago:**
North America, along with Europe and Asia, is part of the Laurasian supercontinent.

▶ **100 million years ago:**
A great sea floods the middle of the continent, dividing it into two **landmasses.**

▶ **95–65 million years ago:**
The Rocky Mountains begin to uplift.

▶ **2 million years ago:**
Ice Age glaciers cover much of the continent.

▶ **30,000–15,000 years ago:**
First humans enter North America from Asia.

The Colorado River shaped the deep gorges of the Grand Canyon over millions of years.

Climate, Plants, and Animals

A temperate climate

North America has every kind of **climate**, from frozen **polar** lands to steamy tropics. Most of the continent is in the **temperate** zone, where it never stays too hot or too cold. Although North America has lots of rainfall, it does have some large desert regions. The deserts in the West can be very hot in the day, but very cold at night, especially during the winter months. Even colder are the polar deserts of the continent's arctic north. Polar deserts are covered with little more than ice, snow, or rock. They have very little rainfall.

Forests

North America's temperate regions are ideal for the growth of forests. Common trees are evergreen **conifers**—such as pine, fir, and cedar—and broad-leaved **deciduous** trees—such as oak, maple, and hickory. North America also has rain forests in **tropical** Central America. Huge areas of the continent's forests still remain standing in national parks that are protected from logging.

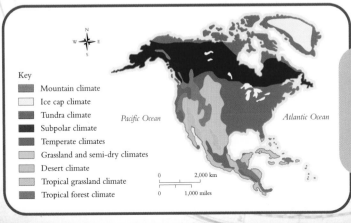

North America has some of the world's tallest desert plants.

Key
- Mountain climate
- Ice cap climate
- Tundra climate
- Subpolar climate
- Temperate climates
- Grassland and semi-dry climates
- Desert climate
- Tropical grassland climate
- Tropical forest climate

Pacific Ocean   *Atlantic Ocean*

0   2,000 km

0   1,000 miles

Although North America is mainly temperate, it has every kind of climate, from tropics to polar **ice caps.**

Grasslands

Just as important as forests are North America's huge grassland regions, especially on the inland plains. Some native grasses of North America can grow taller than a person. Most of the grassland regions are now used for ranching or farming.

Wildlife

North America has many animals similar to those of the nearest continents. In its northern regions, elk, caribou, wild sheep, bears, foxes, and hares are similar to those of Europe and northern Asia. In its southern regions, armadillos, jaguars, monkeys, and parrots are similar to those of South America. Some of North America's animals, such as the coyote, prairie dog, and **pronghorn,** are found nowhere else in the world. And some of its animals, such as bison and bald eagles, have become seriously threatened because of hunting and land clearing over the past two centuries. Fortunately, many of these animals are now protected in parks and reserves.

Animals and habitats

Temperate forests
- brown bear
- North American black bear
- wolf
- lynx
- wolverine
- mink
- white-tailed deer
- moose
- raccoon
- skunk
- beaver
- muskrat
- porcupine
- red squirrel

Deserts
- bobcat
- kangaroo rat
- sidewinder rattlesnake
- jack rabbit
- peccary
- chuckwalla
- tortoise
- elf owl
- gila monster
- roadrunner

Mountains
- cougar
- Rocky Mountain goat
- bighorn sheep
- Dall sheep

Grasslands
- coyote
- bison
- pronghorn
- mule deer
- prairie dog
- pocket gopher
- prairie falcon
- prairie chicken
- rattlesnake

Tropical Central America
- spidermonkey
- howler monkey
- jaguar
- coati
- kinkajou
- peccary

Polar regions
- polar bear
- wolf
- seal
- caribou
- musk ox
- snowy owl

North American forests are often a mixture of conifers and deciduous trees. These temperate forests are an important habitat for many animals.

History and Culture

It is believed that the first people to enter North America came from prehistoric Asia thousands of years ago. They became known as Native Americans, or American Indians, and Inuits, or Eskimos. Some of their groups settled in one place. They lived in villages, farms, or cities. Others were more nomadic, meaning that they traveled from camp to camp, hunting and gathering food in different places.

Europeans take over

Vikings from Europe began exploring North America around 1000 C.E. By the 1500s, Europeans from Spain, France, and England were exploring and settling the continent. Many people came to the continent in search of land and valuable minerals. Others came simply because they were tired of living under the harsh laws of European rulers. Europeans spread throughout the continent, bringing their languages, religions, and customs wherever they went.

Disease and fighting killed many of the Native Americans. It wasn't long before the Europeans forced people from Africa to come to North America. People from other continents also came to North America. Today, the human population of North America is made up of people from all over the world, of many different **cultures,** religions, and language groups. Many people living in North America can trace their family's history to other countries.

As North America grew, the people living there began creating political boundaries and the continent's independent **nations** emerged.

North Americans come from a wide range of cultural backgrounds.

Cultural regions

North America has two main cultural regions. One region, called Anglo-America, includes the United States and Canada. Most people in Anglo-America speak English and have a high **standard of living.** Anglo-American families are not generally as closely knit as families in the rest of the Americas. When children grow up, many of them live and work far away from their parents, brothers, and sisters.

The other region is made up of Mexico, Central America, and many nearby islands. Most people there speak Spanish and their culture is similar to that in South America. The standard of living is not as high as in Anglo-America. Family members are generally very close.

Most people in Mexico and Central America have a culture similar to that of South America.

Facts about living in **North America**

- Many North Americans have **ancestors** who were Native Americans, Europeans, or Africans—or a mixture of these groups.
- **Christianity** and **Judaism** are the main religions of North America.
- North America manufactures more products than any other continent, except Europe.
- The United States and Canada are among countries with the most highly developed transportation and communication systems in the world.

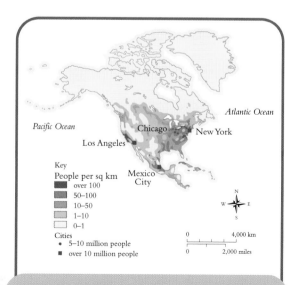

Key
People per sq km
- over 100
- 50–100
- 10–50
- 1–10
- 0–1

Cities
- 5–10 million people
- over 10 million people

Pacific Ocean

Atlantic Ocean

Chicago
New York
Los Angeles
Mexico City

0   4,000 km
0   2,000 miles

North America has the fourth-largest population of the continents.

Introducing
SOUTH AMERICA

South America is the fourth-largest continent. It forms the largest part of Latin America, the region of the Americas where most people speak Spanish or Portuguese. The continent is almost completely surrounded by water. It is linked with North America only by the narrow **Isthmus of Panama.**

South America is a continent of great environmental and **cultural** contrasts. It is a land of snowy peaks, **tropical** rain forests, **fertile plains,** parched deserts, and cold, wind-swept islands. In South America, extremely rich people often live alongside extremely poor people. Its modern cities contrast with tiny Native American villages. Most of South America is not thickly populated. There are twelve countries in South America and three territories, or places ruled by a government in another country.

South America has the world's largest rain forest, the Amazon Basin; the longest mountain chain, the Andes Mountains; the tallest waterfall, Salto Angel, or Angel Falls; and one of the driest deserts, the Atacama Desert. South America has some of the most spectacular scenery in the world. It has great **natural resources,** including water, soil, **timber,** and minerals.

Caracas
VENEZUELA
GUYANA
SURINAM
FRENCH GUIANA
COLOMBIA
ECUADOR
Atlantic
Ocean
BRAZIL
Lima
PERU
Pacific
Ocean
BOLIVIA
PARAGUAY
CHILE
URUGUAY
Santiago
Buenos Aires
ARGENTINA

N
W E
S

0
5,000 km
0
3,000 miles

South America is a colorful mix of countries and cultures.

South America:
facts and figures

Area: 6.9 million sq mi (18 million sq km)

Climate: tropical and **temperate,** with large mountainous areas and rain forests

Population: 355,418,000

Biggest country: Brazil—3.3 million sq mi (8.5 million sq km)

Highest peak: Mt. Aconcagua—22,835 ft (6,960 m)

Lowest point: Peninsula Valdés—131 ft (40 m) below sea level

Largest freshwater lake: Lake Titicaca— 3,205 sq mi (8,300 sq km)

Longest river: Amazon River—4,039 mi (6,500 km)

Biggest desert: Patagonian Desert, Argentina—260,000 sq mi (673,000 sq km)

Crop products: coffee, cocoa, cotton, rubber, soybeans, sugar, bananas, oranges, corn, wheat

Animals and animal products: beef cattle, sheep, wool, fish and fish products

Mineral products: petroleum and related products, natural gas, coal, bauxite, copper, tin, silver, gold, iron ore, zinc, lead, gemstones

Manufactured products: chemicals, furniture, processed foods, clothing and textiles, motor vehicles, aircraft, electronics, furniture, weapons

Venezuela's Angel Falls, the tallest waterfall in the world, is 3,212 feet (979 meters) high.

South American cowboys called gauchos raise cattle on the plains of Argentina.

Landforms

As with North America, South America is shaped like a giant triangle. The western part of South America has the highest mountains and driest deserts, with lower mountains and plains to the east. The **tropical** northern coast of South America is where some of the continent's biggest rivers drain into the sea, including the Amazon River. The great landforms of South America are difficult for humans to cross. This often causes some communities to be **isolated** from others.

Mountains

The Andes Mountains are a great S-shaped chain of mountains on the western side of South America. The Andes run for more than 4,350 miles (7,000 kilometers) along the western edge of the continent. The Andes are ten to fifteen million years old and are still being shaped by volcanoes and **glaciers.** Only the Himalayas of Asia are higher. People of the Andes live on the slopes and in the many valleys and high plains between the peaks. Cities of this region are among the highest in the world. Other highland regions lie in the eastern part of South America. These are older and more worn down than the Andes.

The southern Andes is one of the coldest and stormiest regions of South America.

South American rivers provide important transportation routes in areas where building roads is difficult.

Lowlands

Most of South America is made up of lowland regions, such as rolling hills and broad river valleys. Some of the lowlands are covered with thick rain forest, while others support only small trees, bushes, or grass. One of South America's most **fertile** plains is the Pampas region in the southeast. The Pampas is almost completely flat and has rich grasslands ideal for grazing cattle.

Rivers and rain forests

The Amazon River is the second-longest river in the world. It begins high in the Andes Mountains, fed by hundreds of mountain streams. It flows from the mountains across a low, tropical rain forest, all the way across the continent to the coast of the Atlantic Ocean. Along its course, the Amazon picks up and carries more water than any other river in the world. It pours so much water into the Atlantic Ocean that the water far out into the ocean has the muddy yellow color of the river. Other major South American rivers include the Orinoco, Parana, Paraguay, São Francisco, Negro, and Uruguay.

Diary of a continent

▶ **200 million years ago**
South America is part of the Gondwana supercontinent, along with Africa, Australia, and Antarctica.

▶ **150 million years ago**
Gondwana breaks up.

▶ **45 million years ago**
South America is an island continent, cut off from all the others.

▶ **10–15 million years ago**
The Andes Mountains begin to uplift.

▶ **3 million years ago**
North America and South America are connected by the **Isthmus** of Panama.

▶ **2 million–10,000 years ago**
Ice Age glaciers cover the southern tip of Chile and Argentina.

▶ **30 000–12 000 years ago**
Humans enter North and South America from Asia on the Bering Land Bridge.

The driest deserts of South America lie on the western side of the Andes Mountains. There are also large, dry regions on the southeastern tip of the continent.

Climate, Plants, and Animals

The largest part of South America lies in the tropics. This means that most of the continent has warm to hot weather throughout the year, usually with plenty of rain. About a third of the continent is covered with **tropical** rain forests. More than 2,000 different kinds of trees live in the rain forests, along with many other native plants and animals.

Forests in danger

Rain forest plants are a valuable **natural resource** for **timber,** chemicals, medicine, and food. The green leaves of rain forest plants produce large amounts of oxygen, which improves the quality of Earth's air. However, huge areas of rain forest are being cleared away, so the land can be used for ranches or farms. When the thick vegetation is cleared, there is little to protect the land from heavy rains and much of the valuable soil is washed away. The land can only be saved by replanting trees.

The temperate zone

Not all of South America is warm and rainy. Its high peaks are mainly cold and its deserts are mainly dry, even those in the tropical zone. South America is very long, and its narrow southern tip reaches far into the cooler **temperate** zone. This region lies closer to Antarctica than any other continent. It is less than 620 miles (1,000 kilometers) away. For this reason, South America is often used as a base for Antarctic expeditions.

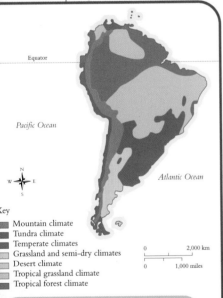

Equator

Pacific Ocean

Atlantic Ocean

N
W   E
S

Key
- Mountain climate
- Tundra climate
- Temperate climates
- Grassland and semi-dry climates
- Desert climate
- Tropical grassland climate
- Tropical forest climate

0   2,000 km
0   1,000 miles

The largest part of South America lies in the tropics, but the **climate** varies greatly across the continent.

Many rain forest animals have grasping claws and tails for climbing trees.

Wildlife

A wide variety of animals live in South America. Some of these, such as llamas, alpacas, and large rodents such as the **cavy** and **capybara,** are native only to this continent. The rain forests have the greatest variety of animals. Many of them are climbers—monkeys, sloths, opossums, and **kinkajous**—with grasping claws or tails. On the ground are animals such as **tapirs,** anteaters, and army ants. Many rain forest animals, such as certain snakes, lizards, and the water opossum, can both climb and swim. Amazon waters are home to **manatees,** catfish, lungfish, electric eels, and deadly piranha fish.

There are more kinds of birds in South America than in any other continent. A wide variety of colorful toucans, parrots, and hummingbirds live in the tropics. The giant condor lives in the mountains and the ostrich-like rhea on the Pampas. Many seabirds live along the South American coast.

Animals and habitats

Islands
- Galapagos tortoise
- lava lizard
- marine iguana
- flightless cormorant
- tree finch
- ground finch

Grasslands and dry regions
- maned wolf
- Pampas fox
- tuco-tuco
- Pampas guinea pig
- mara
- Pampas deer
- giant anteater
- nine-banded armadillo
- fairy armadillo
- rhea
- burrowing owl

Mountains
- llama (domesticated)
- vicuña
- guanaco
- chinchilla
- condor
- Andean flamingo
- Chilean parakeet
- Darwin's frog

Tropical forests and rivers
- jaguar
- spider monkey
- howler monkey
- tapir
- sloth
- capybara
- vampire bat
- ocelot
- kinkajou
- coati
- woolly opossum
- water opossum
- paca
- peccary
- Amazon dolphin
- manatee
- toucan
- caiman
- anaconda
- poison arrow frog
- piranha

Llamas and alpacas are camel-like animals of the Andes Mountains. People who live in the mountains use these animals for carrying heavy loads and for wool.

History and Culture

The first people to live in South America were American Indians. It is believed that they entered South America from North America thousands of years ago. They crossed over on the **Isthmus** of Panama and spread into all regions of the continent, from the **tropical** rain forest in the north to the stormy southern tip. Many South American Indians hunted and gathered their food. Others grew crops such as squash and beans. Some, such as the Inca, lived in large communities. The Inca ruled over a great empire in the Andes Mountains. They built temples, roads, bridges, and irrigation systems for watering crops. They also used pottery, metals, woven cloth, and **domestic animals.**

European invasion

Europeans began arriving in South America during the 1500s. Most of them were from Spain or Portugal. They conquered the American Indians they met, including the great Inca Empire. They began to settle the land, establishing mines and farms, and forcing American Indians to work as slaves. More slaves were brought in from Africa. The slaves were later freed, but they remained much poorer than Europeans in South America. European settlements steadily grew into modern **nations** such as Brazil, Peru, Bolivia, and Chile. Many of them fought wars to gain their independence from European rule. South American countries are democracies, meaning that society is governed by elected officials. However, many have been ruled by **military dictators.**

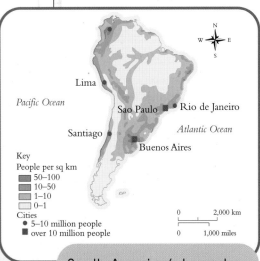

South America's largest population centers grew from European settlements.

Isolation

Many regions of South America are still **isolated** from one another. Transportation and communication have often been limited by the many natural barriers—mountains, deserts, swamps, and rain forests—between the different regions. There are some roads and railways through these natural barriers, but many people still rely on animals, boats, or airplanes to travel.

Culture

South America is part of Latin America. It has a similar **culture** to Central America. Most of the people speak Spanish or Portuguese. The people in South America take great pride in their traditional arts, crafts, music, and folklore. Family members are very close, with parents, children, grandparents, uncles, aunts, cousins, and other relatives living nearby or in the same house. Poverty is a problem for many South Americans, even in the wealthier countries of Argentina, Brazil, Uruguay, and Venezuela.

Facts about living in South America

- Like North Americans, most South Americans have **ancestors** who were Native Americans, Europeans, or Africans—or a mixture of these groups.
- Most South Americans live in cities. Some of the cities are very large, such as Rio de Janeiro and São Paulo in Brazil, or Buenos Aires in Argentina.
- Most towns and cities of South America lie on or near the coast.
- **Christianity** is the main religion in South America, and most people follow the Catholic religion.

South Americans take great pride in their traditional arts and crafts.

Continental Connections and
PLATE TECTONICS

North America and South America are joined together by a land bridge. This land bridge—the narrow **Isthmus** of Panama—allows plants, animals, and people to **migrate** from one continent to the other. Without this connection, North America and South America would be separated from each other. They would probably have completely different kinds of wildlife and human **cultures.** Other land connections occurred in ancient times. For example, North America was once connected to Europe, and South America was once connected to Africa.

Origin of land bridges

The Isthmus of Panama was not always there. Scientists believe it was formed around three million years ago. Before this time, North America and South America were separate continents and had very different kinds of living things. So what caused the Isthmus of Panama to appear? What causes any land bridge to appear—or to disappear? These questions puzzled scientists for many years. They finally found the answers through the concept of plate **tectonics.**

False ideas

Before the mid–1900s, most people had a false idea about the continents. They believed that the continents stood motionless on Earth, and had been in the same place for billions of years. About 50 years ago, scientists discovered that the continents were moving. In fact, they moved great distances during ancient times, and are still moving today.

Mesosaurus was a crocodile-like reptile that once lived in South America and Africa 250 million years ago, when the two continents were joined.

Giant plates

Scientists learned that the continents were attached to huge plates of rock, called tectonic plates. Together, the different plates make up the surface of Earth, fitting together like a giant jigsaw puzzle. Many plates are larger than the continents, because they contain large sections of Earth's **crust,** including the ocean floor.

Despite their large size, tectonic plates move. They travel very slowly—about four inches (ten centimeters) every year—but they can cover great distances over millions of years. The idea of how plates move is called plate tectonics. Plate tectonics helps us understand the changing position of continents, and how land bridges are formed.

Plates in motion

Tectonic plates are made up of rock from Earth's crust and upper **mantle.** Each plate is about 60 miles (100 kilometers) thick. The plates are rigid, meaning that they are solid and unbreakable. They float on a layer of rocks, moving sideways along a hot lower surface. When the plates move, anything attached to them moves as well, including continents and parts of the ocean floor. They move very slowly, but can cover great distances over time.

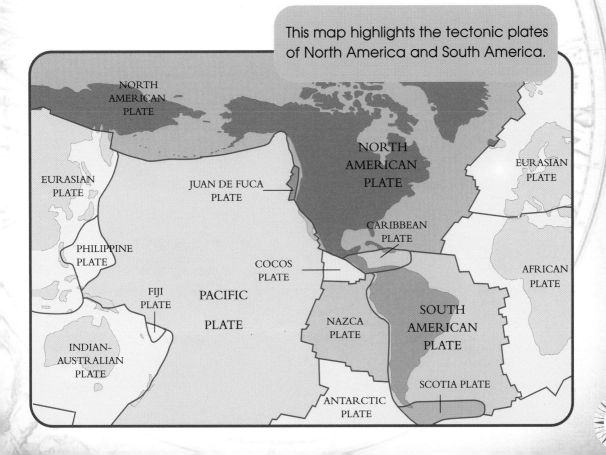

This map highlights the tectonic plates of North America and South America.

NORTH AMERICAN PLATE

NORTH AMERICAN PLATE

EURASIAN PLATE

EURASIAN PLATE

JUAN DE FUCA PLATE

PHILIPPINE PLATE

CARIBBEAN PLATE

AFRICAN PLATE

COCOS PLATE

FIJI PLATE

PACIFIC PLATE

NAZCA PLATE

SOUTH AMERICAN PLATE

INDIAN-AUSTRALIAN PLATE

SCOTIA PLATE

ANTARCTIC PLATE

Plate **tectonics** help us understand how the continents slowly move across Earth's surface. When two continents move close enough to each other, they are likely to form some kind of connection such as a land bridge.

A land bridge is often simply a narrow neck of land such as an **isthmus.** But there are connecting areas that are much bigger and wider than this. In fact, sometimes two continents are pushed right up against each other into one continuous, connecting **landmass.** Europe is connected to Asia in this way. When continents form an even larger landmass, they become one, larger continent. This is why Europe together with Asia is sometimes called Eurasia.

Ancient supercontinents

Today, Europe and Asia are the only continents pushed together to form one landmass. However, tectonic plates have been drifting around the planet for billions of years and all the continents have been pushed together at one time or another. The enormous landmass that formed as the plates carried several continents together is called a supercontinent.

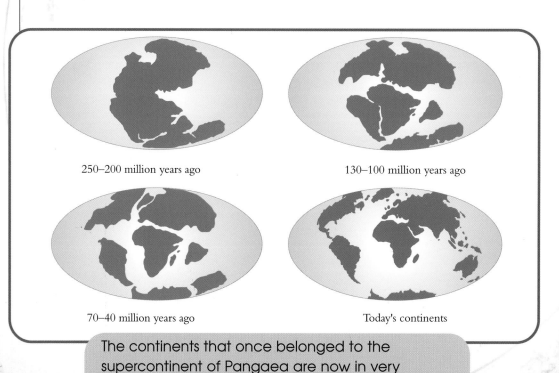

250–200 million years ago

130–100 million years ago

70–40 million years ago

Today's continents

The continents that once belonged to the supercontinent of Pangaea are now in very different positions.

Pangaea

About 250 million years ago, all Earth's continents were pushed together into a supercontinent called Pangaea. It was possible for many kinds of prehistoric plants and animals to spread around to most of the different continents because they were all on a single landmass. The Americas as we know them today did not exist then. North America, Europe, and Asia belonged to the northern part of the supercontinent—called Laurasia. South America, Africa, Australia, and Antarctica belonged to the southern part of the supercontinent—called Gondwana.

Ancient climates

North America and South America had extremely different climates around 280 million years ago. Most of North America and other Laurasian continents had a warm, rainy climate, covered with **tropical** swamps. At the same time, South America was positioned closer to the South Pole. South America and other Gondwanan continents had a colder, drier climate, and huge **glaciers** began to cover much of the landscape.

Break-up and isolation

By 200 million years ago, the plates below Pangaea were causing it to break apart. Laurasia and Gondwana became two smaller supercontinents. Since Laurasia and Gondwana were separate landmasses, wildlife could no longer move from one to the other. By 150 million years ago, the two supercontinents were breaking up into the single continents we know today, including North America and South America. Although North America remained close to other continents, South America drifted completely away and remained distant for millions of years.

Long ago, the Appalachian Mountains of North America connected with the mountains of Europe, when these two continents were a single landmass.

Land Bridges:
THE NARROW LINK

Today, few of the continents are closely connected. Most of them are entirely—or almost entirely—surrounded by water. Land connections between continents are mainly narrow ones, such as an **isthmus.** Even narrow land bridges can make a big difference in the wildlife of a continent, however.

North American links

The great supercontinents of Laurasia and Gondwana began breaking apart during the **Age of Reptiles,** around 200 million years ago. Most of the individual continents were separate by the beginning of the **Age of Mammals,** which started about 65 million years ago. Some continents still remained near others. For example, North America was still near Europe and Asia. This made it possible for land connections to remain and ancient wildlife to migrate between these continents. Prehistoric cats, bears, horses, deer, tapirs, camels, and elephants were some of the mammals that were shared by North America and Eurasia during this time.

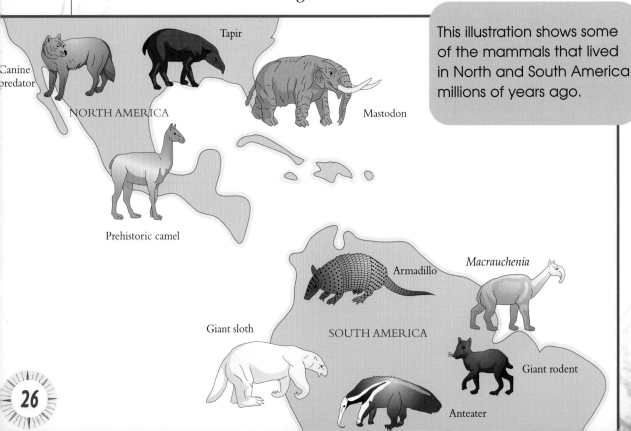

Canine predator

Tapir

NORTH AMERICA

Mastodon

Prehistoric camel

This illustration shows some of the mammals that lived in North and South America millions of years ago.

Armadillo

Macrauchenia

Giant sloth

SOUTH AMERICA

Giant rodent

Anteater

Isolation

Not all continents were close to other continents during the Age of Mammals. South America became an island continent, meaning that it was entirely surrounded by water. Many of the animals that developed in South America at this time were found nowhere else in the world. These included mammals such as sloths, armadillos, giant anteaters, and certain meat-eating **marsupials.** There were also strange-looking mammals unlike any living today, including a camel-like creature with a trunk like an elephant. These animals are now extinct.

Wildlife migrations

South America did not remain an island continent. Late in the Age of Mammals, the drifting plates below North America and South America began to bring these two continents closer together. Around three million years ago, the southern tip of North America touched the northern coast of South America, and a land bridge was formed. It became the Isthmus of Panama. This enabled certain South American mammals to migrate into North America, including armadillos, anteaters, tree sloths, and huge prehistoric ground sloths. The land bridge also enabled certain North American mammals—including cats, bears, deer, **tapirs,** and the camel-like ancestors of llamas—to migrate into South America. The same land bridge would later be crossed by humans.

South American marsupials

More marsupials live in Australia than any other continent, but many prehistoric marsupials lived in ancient South America. The largest of these South American marsupials were **predators.** One of them was as big as a tiger and had a pair of long, curved fangs (similar to the saber-toothed cats of ancient North America). There were also many kinds of opossums. Opossums still live in many parts of North America and South America.

Cougars are large cats that crossed the Isthmus of Panama and are now found throughout the Americas.

Land Bridges:
DROPPING SEAS

In order to form a land bridge, two continents must be close to each other. But sometimes a land bridge also depends on other conditions, such as the level of the sea.

The continental shelf

A land bridge might also depend on where a continent ends. A continent does not simply end where its land meets the ocean. Beyond the shore lies a part of the seafloor called the continental shelf. It is covered by shallow water and is considered part of the continent. The width of the continental shelf can vary greatly. In some places it is very narrow; in other places it reaches far into the sea. Beyond the continental shelf, a slanting surface called the continental slope leads down to the ocean floor.

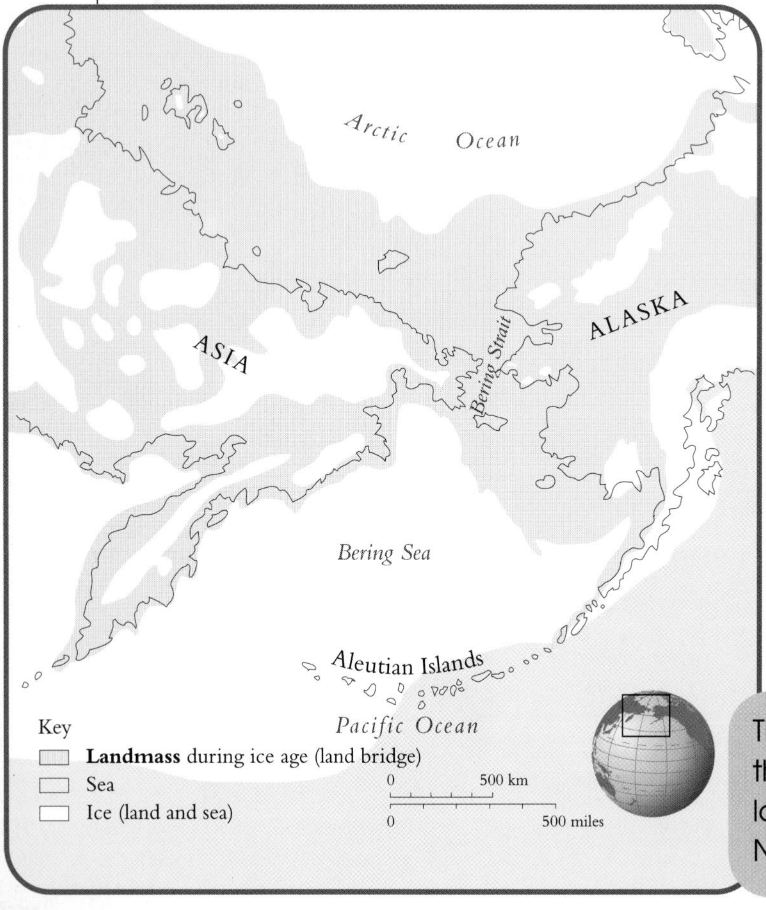

Dropping seas

Sometimes the oceans flood over the continents. This is likely to happen when Earth's **climate** is very warm, causing the **polar ice caps** to melt and the seas to flood into low-lying areas of land. The continents have been flooded in this way many times over the past 500 million years.

Arctic Ocean

ASIA

Bering Strait

ALASKA

Bering Sea

Aleutian Islands

Pacific Ocean

Key
- Landmass during ice age (land bridge)
- Sea
- Ice (land and sea)

0   500 km
0   500 miles

The seas were much lower during the last Ice Age. As a result, a land bridge appeared between North America and Asia.

At other times, the sea level drops and the continental shelves become exposed, increasing the land surface. This is likely to happen when Earth's climate is much colder, causing ice caps to form again and the seas to retreat from low areas of land and even from the continental shelves. This is what happened many thousands of years ago, during the **Ice Age.** Where the exposed continental shelves reach out far enough to connect two different continents, they form a land bridge.

The Bering Land Bridge

The narrow part of the sea that lies between Asia and North America is called the Bering Strait. There is no deep ocean floor below the Bering Strait because it is the place where two continental shelves come together. Between 15,000 and 30,000 years ago, the sea level had dropped far enough to turn this continental shelf into dry land. The Bering Strait became a land bridge. The first people to enter North America came from Asia across this land bridge. It probably took them a week to travel the distance of about 50 miles (80 kilometers). By the end of the last Ice Age, around 10,000 years ago, the sea level rose once more and the Bering Land Bridge was again flooded to become the Bering Strait. By this time, many people had already settled in the Americas.

Land bridges
across the world

It is believed that the first humans lived in Africa. They crossed land bridges into most of the continents. First they migrated into Asia and Europe, which formed a continuous **landmass** with Africa. When continental shelves were exposed during the last Ice Age, humans could cross the Bering Land Bridge from Asia into the Americas. Humans could also cross similar land bridges joining other continents. Antarctica was the only continent too far away to be reached by humans during the last Ice Age.

Navajo and Anasazi **petroglyphs** on the walls of a canyon in Arizona give proof of prehistoric life in the area.

GLOSSARY

Age of Mammals time in Earth's history from about 65 million years ago to the present when mammals became the most common animals

Age of Reptiles time in Earth's history about 250 to 65 million years ago when reptiles such as dinosaurs were the largest living animals

ancestor one from whom a person is descended

capybara large South American rodent that can grow up to four feet (1.2 meters) long

cavy plant-eating rodent from South America

Christianity Christian religion, based on the teachings of Jesus

civilization stage of cultural development at which writing and the keeping of written records is attained

climate kind of weather that occurs in a particular region

conifer non-flowering tree or shrub that has cones and needles

crust Earth's outermost rock layer, about 5 to 45 miles (8 to 70 kilometers) thick

culture ideas, skills, arts, and way of life of a certain group of people. Something that has to do with culture is called cultural.

deciduous sheds its leaves in the fall

domestic animals tame animals that are useful to humans

exposed laid open to sun, wind, and rain

fertile rich in nutrients

glacier mass of ice that moves slowly across the land

ice age time when parts of Earth become colder and are covered by glaciers. There have been many ice ages, but the most recent Ice Age ended over 10,000 years ago.

ice cap permanent covering of ice

iron ore mineral mined for the iron it contains

isolated set apart from others

isthmus narrow strip of land connecting two larger areas

Judaism Jewish religion, based on the Torah, or Old Testament

kinkajou slender, yellow-brown mammals related to raccoons

landmass large area of land, such as a continent

manatees large water mammals, sometimes called sea cows, with flippers and a flat, oval tail

mantle layer of rock about 1,800 miles (2,900 kilometers) thick that lies below Earth's crust

marsupial mammal that carries its young in a pouch

migrate   to move from one area to another

military dictator   member of the armed forces who rules a country with complete power

nation   country or kingdom; people with a common government

natural resource   supply of useful material from nature

peccary   pig-like mammal of the Americas

petroglyph   rock drawing or carving made by people from long ago

plain   area of land that is mostly treeless

polar   of the Arctic or Antarctic regions

predator   animals that hunts, kills, and eats other animals

pronghorn   antelope-like mammal with horns and hooves

sorghum   tall cereal plant used for feeding livestock or making products such as molasses and syrup

standard of living   level of goods and income enjoyed by a society

tapir   large, pig-like mammal related to the horse and rhinoceros

tectonic   relating to the structure and changes in Earth's crust

temperate   moderate; not permanently hot or cold

timber   trees or forested land; wood used for constructing buildings, furniture and wooden objects

tropical   of the tropics, the warm regions around the equator

Vikings   pirates, warriors and explorers from Scandinavia who invaded many parts of Europe from the 700s to 900s

FURTHER READING

Petersen, David. *Africa.* Danbury, Conn.: Children's Press, 1998.

Petersen, David. *Antarctica.* Danbury, Conn.: Children's Press, 1998.

Petersen, David. *Asia.* Danbury, Conn.: Children's Press, 1998.

Petersen, David. *Australia.* Danbury, Conn.: Children's Press, 1998.

Petersen, David. *Europe.* Danbury, Conn.: Children's Press, 1998.

Petersen, David. *North America.* Danbury, Conn.: Children's Press, 1998.

Petersen, David. *South America.* Danbury, Conn.: Children's Press, 1998.

INDEX